Nelson Grammar

Denis and Helen Ballance

Book 1

Contents

Introduction

Grammar is the name given to the rules for writing and speaking English. Because English is spoken in so many parts of the world, it is important that everyone who uses it should keep to the same rules.

Nelson Grammar is a series of books which sets out to explain some of the rules of grammar. The rules given in this book have been chosen because they are the ones you need to know at this stage of your school life. As well as rules dealing with such things as capital letters, punctuation and word order, the books introduce and explain some of the special words used in grammar.

Nelson Grammar is designed to be used alongside your other work in language. Each page spotlights a single grammar topic and is intended to provide the central point for one week's work.

Read the rules and examples given in the pink patch at the top of each page first. After you have studied the rules carefully, do the exercises which provide practice in applying them. Here and there, you will find 'Just for fun' and Revision pages.

At the end of the book, there is an index to help you to look up topics you may need when you are writing. Please do not write the answers to the puzzles and exercises in this book.

Capital letters and small letters

The capital letters are: A B C D E F G H I J K L M N O P Q R S T U V W X Y Z

The small letters are: a b c d e f g h i j k l m n o p q r s t u v w x y z

Most words are written in small letters.

Some words, usually on notices, are written in capital letters.

Some special names have a single capital at the beginning.

A

1 Write the fifteen capital letters, like A, that are made up of straight lines.

2 Write the seven small letters that have tall stems above the line, like b.

B These words are written in three different ways. Write the two in each set that are correct.

1 happy   HAPPY   haPPy

2 Paper   paPer   paper

3 LIGHTS   Lights   liGhts

4 Night   nighT   NIGHT

5 Bath   bath   BaTH

6 THiN   thin   Thin

C All the words starting with capital letters in these sentences are special names. Write them in two lists, headed PEOPLE and PLACES.

Tom and Mary were born in Blackpool and lived in Liverpool for a time. Redhill is now their home. Harry Brown, their father, works in London but he visits Brighton, Reading and Portsmouth every week.

Copy these shapes. Add one straight line to make each one into a capital letter.

The alphabet

Every word is made up of one or more letters of the alphabet.

Learn the order in which the letters are arranged.

You may find it helpful to learn them in groups.

a b c d e f g   h i j k l m   n o p q r s t   u v w x y z

A Write the letter that:

1 comes before d.
2 follows t.
3 comes before j.

4 comes before o.
5 follows p.
6 comes before m.

7 comes before z.
8 follows d.
9 comes before g.

B Write the missing letters from these alphabets to make words.

1 a – c d – f g h i j k – m n o p q r s – u v w x y z

2 a b c – e f g h – j k l m n o p q – s – u v w x – z

3 a b c d e f – – i j k l m n – p q r – – u v w x y z

Here is a code. Each number stands for the letter written above it.

a	b	c	d	e	f	g	h	i	j	k	l	m	n	o	p	q	r	s	t	u	v	w
1	2	3	4	5	6	7	8	9	10	11	12	13	14	15	16	17	18	19	20	21	22	23

The names of these things are given in the code. What are they?

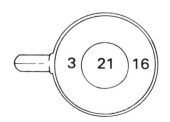

3 21 16

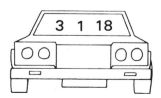

3 1 18

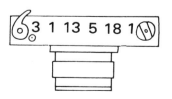

3 1 13 5 18 1

5

Alphabetical order

All the words in a dictionary are placed in alphabetical order.

Words starting with **a** are all together at the front of the dictionary.

The words that begin with **b** come next and so on through the alphabet to **z.**

A This set of words is in alphabetical order: actor   bring   carry   duster

Write these sets of words in alphabetical order.

1 bat cat eel ape dog   4 ten vex use ran sat

2 jar kid fan hut ink   5 hay fig bun ant tea

3 now old pip lit may   6 pen yes run zoo sun

B Write these lists of names which are in alphabetical order. Fill in the spaces with other names.

  Ann   B——   C——   Diane   Eve   F——   G——   H——

I——   J——   Kate   L——   M——   Naomi   O——

P——   No Q   R——   S——   T——   Una   V——

  Andrew —— —— —— Edward —— —— Hugh

—— —— —— —— —— —— Owen ——

Quintin —— —— —— No U —— —— No X Y Z

Put these words in alphabetical order to make a sentence to fit the picture.

cowboy   home   geese

drove   A   big   fat

eight

Sentences

This is a sentence.

My coat keeps me warm.

The sentence is about a coat.

The sentence tells you what the coat does.

A Write the one word that tells you what each of these sentences is about.

1 Dogs like to eat bones.

2 The rabbit is eating a carrot.

3 My brother has curly hair.

4 Elephants have thick skins.

5 Peter has broken a window.

6 Birds build their nests in spring.

7 Snow blocked all the roads.

8 Tall trees sway in the wind.

9 Nine little mice sat in the sun.

10 Bright sunshine makes me sneeze.

B How many sentences are there here?

A dark cloud hid the moon. Gentle waves lapped the shore. Slowly, the boat drifted in towards the island. It touched the beach. Three shadowy figures slipped over the side. The raid had begun at last!

Put these words in order to make sentences to fit the pictures.

windows house this
door a four and has

middle spider sits
of the in web the
its waiting

Sentences: capital letters and full stop

| A sentence always begins with a capital letter. | A sentence always ends with a full stop. | **Example:** Sheep have woolly coats. |

A Write each of these sentences again. Make the first letter a capital and put a full stop at the end.

1   mary is playing a recorder

2   the shop is closed all day

3   owls nest in hollow trees

4   night always follows day

5   my new shoes are brown

6   grandma has gone to sleep

B There are four pairs of sentences below. Write them correctly by putting in full stops and capital letters where they are needed.

Example:

The wind is in the north we shall have snow before dawn → The wind is in the north. We shall have snow before dawn.

1   turn left when you come to the road the farm is near the wood

2   we saw the girls earlier they were going for a long walk

3   strong winds blew all night a ship sank in the bay

4   the road through the wood is blocked a tree has fallen down

Follow the arrows to find out about these pictures.

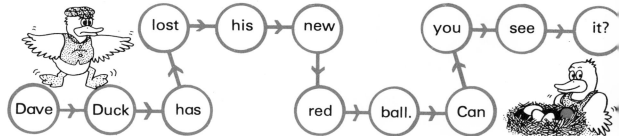

8

Sentences: making sense

A sentence has to make sense.

This is a sentence.

In April the buds begin to grow.

This is not a sentence.

In April the sunny days.

A Write these sentences. Add one word to each to make it complete.

1 Jill wore her new ——.
2 On Saturdays we buy ——.
3 They both fell into the ——.
4 Horses like to eat ——.
5 The dog chased the cat ——.

6 —— swing from tree to tree.
7 —— usually have four wheels.
8 —— are made of bricks.
9 —— school we went home.
10 —— we must wear raincoats.

B Write these sentences. Choose the word from the brackets that makes the best sense to fill the space.

1 The water is too —— for paddling. (wet   deep   salty)
2 Susan trapped her hand in the ——. (flowers   custard   door)
3 A —— fell into the pot of plum jam. (lion   fly   bus)
4 They were playing —— in the shed. (cards   football   cricket)
5 The —— fish jumped over the waterfall. (fried   silver   frozen)

Write a sentence about each picture.

9

Nouns

A noun is a name word.

Many nouns are names of things you can see and touch.

clock
hand
case

A Look around the room. Write the names of ten things you can see.

B Pick out the nouns from this list. Write them in your book.

book   read   page   bird   soft   rock   make   door

paid   sees   deer   know   wall   hair   then   cage

C Copy this writing. Fill in the spaces with nouns of your own.

As the end of summer draws near, many —— fly away to warmer ——
Their tiny —— carry them across the —— to Africa. Next ——, they
will fly back to build their —— in the —— and hedges of the English
countryside.

Write the word NOUNS in your book. Underneath, make a list of the names of
the things shown in the pictures.

Put the first letters of the nouns together to make two words of five letters each.

Nouns with capital letters: people

If a noun is the name of a person, its first letter must be a capital.

I by itself always has a capital letter.

Example:

John and I saw Elizabeth Raine near the shops.

A Pick out from this list the ten nouns that are names of people. Write them with the first letters as capitals.

jones jean sky caravan robert parton alison weasel bus

time sheep henry susan perry william cottage foggy harris

B Write these sentences. Begin the names of people with capital letters.

1 simon has a sister named deborah.

2 peter has two brothers, paul and jim.

3 lynn's uncle is called will williams.

4 claire harvey is not here today.

5 i went to see susan barker

6 john does not like cabbage

7 In the play, neil is an elf.

8 mary's best friend is kim.

C Take letters from the end of the first word and the beginning of the second to make boys' and girls' first names.

Example: fire guard → fi(re g)uard → Reg

the lender one illness great image tired warders last evening

Can you draw some more capital letter people like these?

Nouns with capital letters: titles

Titles that go with names of people begin with capital letters.

 Miss Smith Mrs Smith Major Smith

A Write these names and titles. Make the first letter of each word a capital.

captain denis heath   sir vincent thompson   sergeant jackson

bishop potterton   lord burwash   lady kenton   prince john

police constable myers   petty officer grey   judge peterson

B Write this sentence. Put in capital letters where they are needed.

the engagement is announced between miss henrietta pugh, only daughter of sir peter and lady pugh of redburn, hampshire and commander anthony wilkins, eldest son of doctor and mrs wilkins of market langley, kent.

C Write these titles in three lists under the headings ROYAL NAVY, ARMY and ROYAL AIR FORCE. Each list should contain four titles.

Colonel   Leading Seaman   Pilot Officer   Squadron Leader

Commander   Air Marshal   Private   Sergeant-Major

Leading Aircraftman   General   Lieutenant-Commander   Rear Admiral

These people have mixed up their hats. Write the number of each hat and its owner's name.

Guardsman Smith   Police Constable Dodd

Ordinary Seaman Williams   Judge Gregory

Bishop Toft   Flight-Sergeant Miller

Nouns: singular and plural

If we are talking about more than one thing, the noun usually has an **s** added.

singular
tree
trees
plural

The form that means one is called the singular.

The form that means more than one is called the plural.

A Write the ten singular (meaning one) nouns in this list.

peg   aeroplane   chairs   pencils   fence   carpets   buckles

boat   goal   buttons   cow   roses   window   lift   egg   ant

B Write these sentences. Each set of brackets (   ) contains a singular and a plural noun. Choose the correct one.

The new (cart   carts) was loaded with (case   cases), (barrel barrels) and (tray   trays). A pair of strong (horse   horses) was harnessed up and the (driver   drivers) cracked his (whip   whips). They set off along the (lane   lanes) leading to the main (road   roads) at a brisk pace.

C All of these words end in s. Write the ten that are plural nouns.

kiss   nails   cross   bus   birds   drums   desks   pass

rivers   hammers   pens   fields   goddess   streets   monkeys

Write a singular noun and a plural noun to fit each pair of pictures.

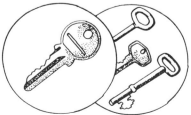

13

Revision

A Write these sets of nouns in alphabetical order.

1 cake apple doughnut bun egg

2 hamster frog impala jackal gnu

3 kite oak lock moss nest

4 Ventnor Rhyl Towyn Urmston Sale

5 prince duke earl queen king

6 tin steel brass zinc gold

B Copy these cards. Put in capital letters where they are needed.

mr mark johnson	admiral sir john lawson	miss sheila morris
lady jane gray	major-general williams	mrs priscilla cook
rev. c. g. hughes	doctor robin price	capt. andrew smith

C Divide this passage into six sentences. Put in capital letters and full stops.

last week, princess alexandra came to open the new airport james and i went to see her it was a damp cold day she was wearing a light blue raincoat and a white hat she was met by lord bolton he was carrying a large umbrella

D Make an alphabetical list of all the nouns you can find in these sentences. Their first letters are given at the end.

The fox lived in an earth under an old larch in the hedge bordering my garden. Its cubs first appeared in late July. I saw them peeping through the ivy surrounding the burrow one afternoon while I was working in the kitchen. They went off hunting along the ditch, looking for mice.

a——	b——	c——	d——	e——	f——	g——
h——	i——	j——	k——	l——	m——	

Just for fun

A Find the name of a part of the body hidden in each of these words.

Example: describes → desc(rib)es → rib

machine   pearl   diagnosed   alarmed   wheels
illegal   slipper   prefaced   chairman   vetoed

B Write letters in place of the squares to make words to fit the pictures.

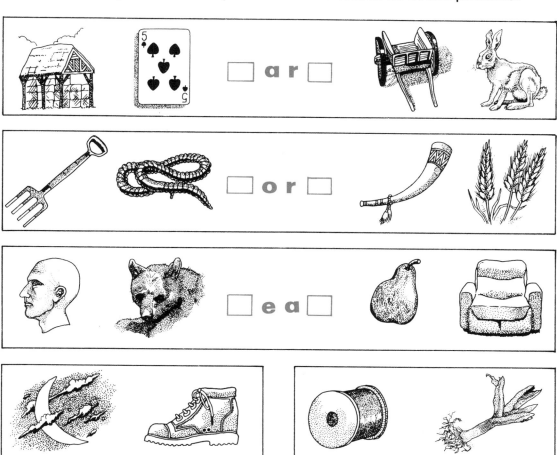

A or an?

The letters below which are in heavy type are called vowels. The rest are consonants.
The letter **y** can be either.

Write **a** before words starting with consonants. Write **an** before words starting with vowels.

a b c d **e** f g h **i** j k l m n **o** p q r s t **u** v w x **(y)** z

A   Write the ten words in this list that start with vowels.

peg   egg   log   ink   arm   owl   bag   ham   urn   rim   day   oak   tin

pig   top   cat   elm   pin   aim   mop   inn   sun   dog   eel   mat   fig

B   Write these sentences. Use a or an to fill the spaces.

1   Mark was walking in — field.   4   It crash landed near — old cast

2   He saw — aeroplane flying low.   5   One of the wings hit — tree.

3   The motor made — odd noise.   6   The pilot broke — bone in his l

C   Make as many words as you can by putting different vowels into these sets of consonants.   **Example:** p – n → pan   pen   pin   pun

b – t   t – p   t – n   p – t   m – st

Put these words in order to make sentences to fit the pictures.

Helen   and
breakfast
grapefruit
had   for
an   egg   a

bath   to   a
elephant
have   An
getting
ready   is

Questions

This is a question mark.

?

It is put at the end of a sentence instead of a full stop to show that a question is being asked.

Example:

Is this the road to Newley?

A A question usually asks for an answer. Five of these sentences are questions. Write the five and put question marks after them.

1 This is Jamie's old jacket.

2 How far is it to Derby, please.

3 Robins stay in Britain all winter.

4 Is your birthday this month.

5 Is Mrs Perry coming today.

6 Why does the wind blow.

B Write the questions to which these could be the answers.

1 My father's name is William.

2 It grows on the backs of sheep.

3 You play it by plucking the strings.

4 She lives in Buckingham Palace.

5 It opens at nine o'clock.

6 I am eight next week.

C Put spaces between these words and add full stops or question marks to make them into sentences.

1 HowmanypeopleliveinBanbury   (one sentence)

2 ThisdoghasbittenmeDoesitbelongtoyou   (two sentences)

Write a question to go in each balloon.

Adjectives

Adjectives are describing words. They tell us more about nouns.

An adjective may be placed next to the word it describes, or it may stand by itself.

Example:

The **new china** plates have **gold** edges. The edges are **gold**.

A   Copy the nouns, which are in red. By each noun, write the adjective that describes it. **Example:** seas – heavy

Heavy seas were breaking over the stone jetty. The battered ship limped through the narrow entrance to the inner harbour. Her captain was exhausted. The brave man had been standing on the open bridge for many hours, steering the stricken ship to a safe mooring.

B   Write these sentences. Choose adjectives of your own to fill the spaces.

The —— sunlight filtered through the —— branches of the —— trees. Two —— deer peered from the —— shade beneath a —— chestnut tree. The larger, a —— buck, took a —— step forward. He paused, listening to the —— sound of a —— dog. The second deer gave him a —— push and they both stepped out into the —— light of the —— clearing.

C   Re-arrange the groups of red letters to make adjectives to fit the nouns that follow them. **Example:** gridvin rain → driving rain

alenc hands   yppha faces   eped water   ystru iron

atll trees   yklis fur   ludo voices   loco drink

Write five adjectives to describe this monster.

Number adjectives

There are two sorts of number adjectives.

One sort tells you **how many** things there are.

Examples: ten horses   fifty men   eight legs

The other sort tells you their **order of place** in a series. These are called ordinal numbers.

Example: This is the tenth house.

A Copy these numbers. Next to each one write the ordinal number that matches it. **Example:** eleven → eleventh

four   six   nine   seven   twelve   fourteen   five   fifteen   two

three   eighteen   eight   one   thirty-two   twenty-one   twenty-three

B Find the number adjectives in these sentences. Write the nouns that go with them.

1   There are five seats in the car.

2   Seven books are still missing.

3   Peter is eight years old today.

4   The third horse has fallen.

5   Of archers there were eighty.

6   The tower is fifty metres high.

7   We saw a thousand birds arrive.

8   A million people live in Glasgow.

Look at the picture, which shows the end of a yacht race. Write the sentences below and fill the spaces with ordinal numbers.

The ——— yacht across the finishing line was K7. K3 came ——— , beating K1 into ——— place in a close finish. K9 was ———. K4 led the tail-enders home to come ———. K2 and K5 were placed ——— and ——— in that order.

Colour adjectives

The names of colours are adjectives. They describe nouns.

Example:

This is her **green** coat.

Her coat is **green**.

A Choose colour adjectives to describe these nouns.

1 —— sand   3 —— grapes   5 —— moss   7 —— buttercups

2 —— corn   4 —— bricks   6 —— fish   8 —— elderberries

B Write these sentences. Choose colour adjectives to fill the spaces.

1 Lisa's skin is as —— as snow but her hair is as —— as coal.

2 At Christmas time, holly has —— berries and —— leaves.

3 The Union Jack, the British flag, is ——, —— and ——.

4 In autumn, the woodland trees are a blaze of —— and ——.

C Write sentences of your own containing these colour names.

orange   grey   silver   pink   purple

Write the colour names given in the red circles. For each one, find two similar names in the black circles and write them underneath.

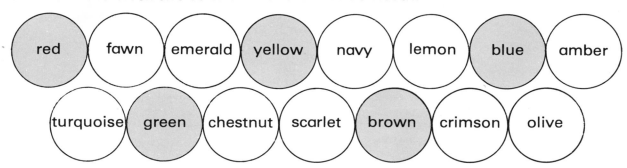

20

Confusing words: to, too, two

to the boats

to: I am going
to bed.
It is five
to four.

too heavy

too: This chair is
too low for me.
We had some
fireworks too.

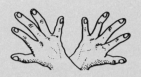

two hands

two: We caught
two fish.
It is half
past two.

A Write these sentences. Fill each space with to, too or two.

1 Tim and I walked — the park.
2 There were — eggs in the nest.
3 The plant is — big for the pot.
4 I was asked — wait outside.

5 We were — late for the bus.
6 He was here — hours ago.
7 Mary thought she saw him —.
8 I should like — have a pony.

B Write to, too or two in place of ... to complete these words and
word groups.

... day   twenty-...   ... pence   ... and fro   ...night

... many cooks spoil the broth.   ...morrow   ...-legged

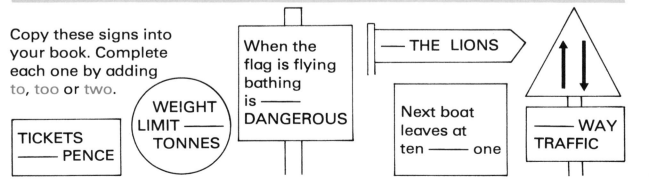

Copy these signs into
your book. Complete
each one by adding
to, too or two.

TICKETS
—— PENCE

WEIGHT
LIMIT ——
TONNES

When the
flag is flying
bathing
is ——
DANGEROUS

—— THE LIONS

Next boat
leaves at
ten —— one

—— WAY
TRAFFIC

Word families

Some words go together in families.

man

father

woman

mother

child

child

A   Choose the word from the brackets that fits in with the family.

1   uncle —— cousin   (mother   aunt   grandmother)

2   drake —— duckling   (goose   duck   swan)

3   bull —— calf   (sow   hind   cow)

4   fox —— cub   (doe   vixen   bitch)

5   gander —— gosling   (swan   goose   duck)

6   cock —— chick   (hen   goose   duck)

B   There are five different families of animals in the box. Sort them out and write them in their families.

Example:

Male	Female	Young
ram	ewe	lamb

dog   piglet   foal   stallion
nanny-goat   puppy   lioness
mare   boar   billy-goat   sow
kid   bitch   lion   cub

Which animal families do these belong to?

cob   cygnet   pen   leveret   doe   buck   buck   doe   fawn

Confusing words: of, off

of means 'belonging to' or 'from among'.

Example:

This cup is part of the new tea set.

off means 'away from', or the opposite of 'on'.

Example:

A branch fell off the elm tree.

A Write of or off to fill the spaces.

1   The Prince — Wales.
2   Take — your shoes.
3   A cup — tea.

4   — and on.
5   The ace — clubs.
6   An early kick —.

7   Two —— them.
8   —— the pitch.
9   Time —— day.

B Write these sentences. Use of or off to fill the spaces.

1   Two players were sent — the field.
2   A wheel fell — his new car.
3   Julie is the captain — the team.

4   They are — to Wales next week.
5   I need a pair — sharp scissors.
6   Carr Lane is — Church Street.

Write a sentence containing of to go in this 'balloon'.

Write a sentence containing off to go in this 'balloon'.

Revision

A Read these sentences and answer the questions below.

The tall masts of the sailing ship creaked under a full spread of heavy sails. A small flag flew at her topmast but the bright light reflected from the sunlit waves made it impossible to tell what it was. Two figures were standing on the high prow of the proud vessel. One of them had long hair and broad shoulders. Suddenly, a shrill voice rang out.
   "Man the guns! It's Amos Duncan, the blackest pirate of them all."

B 1 The red words are nouns. Each one has an adjective to describe it. Write the nouns and the adjectives that describe them in your book.

2 Write the nine singular nouns under the heading SINGULAR.

3 Write the five plural nouns under the heading PLURAL.

4 How many sentences are there in the passage about the pirate ship?

C Write these sentences. Choose the correct words from the brackets.

(A   An) angry sailor ordered the pirates (to   too   two) stand (of   off) from the side (of   off) the ship. (To   Too   Two) members (of   off) Duncan's crew threw (a   an) grappling hook towards our rigging. It was thrown (to   too   two) low and (a   an) sudden gust (of   off) wind drew us clear and caused the hook (to   too   two) slide (of   off) our deck into the sea.

D Write the sentences below that ask questions. Add question marks to those you choose.

Why had the pirates attacked us.   Could we escape.   The ship was heavily loaded.   How far were we from land.   Did they know what we were carrying.

24

Just for fun

A   Write the name of everything beginning with d in this picture.

B   Find the animal's name hidden in each of these words.

     Example: pottering → p(otter)ing → otter

     scattered   scowled   shared   debate   unsealed   lucrative

C   Find the bird's name hidden in each of these words.

     bowler   scooter   smarting   crooked   stitched   disrobing

D   Arrange the letters in these animal and bird shapes to make words describing the sounds they make.

Plurals: words ending in s, ss, x and zz

The plurals of words ending in **s**, **ss**, **x** and **zz** are made by adding **es**.

glass

glasses

box

boxes

A   Write a plural word to fit each picture.

 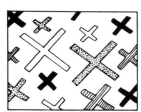 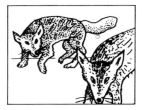 

B   Write these sentences. Change the red words into plurals.

Some class of moss are found growing only in the high pass of the mountains of Iceland. The ground is bare rock and no grass grow there. The pure air, with no trace of harmful gas , allows plants to grow which are found nowhere else on the land mass of the earth. Find Iceland in your atlas.

Make plurals of words ending in ss by writing these letters in front of es.

p	r	i	n	c	e	s	s
	d	u	c	h	e	s	s
			b	o	s	s	
		d	r	e	s	s	
			m	i	s	s	
	h	o	s	t	e	s	s
w	a	i	t	r	e	s	s

es

Join these parts of words to make more plurals.

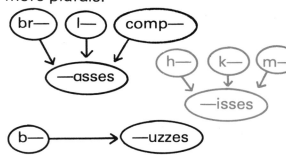

26

Verbs

What is missing from this sentence? **Susan —— home in the rain.**

The missing word should tell you what Susan did.

The missing word could be **ran, came, walked, trudged.**

A Write these sentences. Choose words from the box to fill the spaces.

lived	climbed
stole	stretched
planted	drove
gave	entered

Jack —— the cow to market. A man —— him some magic beans in exchange for it. He —— the beans in the garden. Next morning, the bean plant had grown and —— up to the sky. Jack —— the beanstalk and —— a land of magic. He —— some gold from an ogre. Jack and his mother —— happily ever after.

B Write these sentences. Fill each space with a word of your own.

1   The soldier —— up his gun.

2   Ben —— off his skateboard.

3   A tall tree —— in the garden.

4   Swallows —— away for winter.

5   Our puppy —— up my shoes.

6   Karen —— her bicycle up the road.

Copy this puzzle. Pick out the words from the sentences that tell you what Susan did. Write the words into the puzzle in order. The first letters of the words are written in for you.

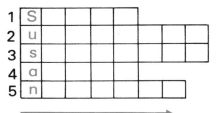

1   Susan shook her umbrella.

2   She unlocked the door with her key.

3   She switched on the television.

4   She asked her mother for a drink.

5   She noticed a letter on the table.

27

Verbs

The word that tells you what is being done in the sentence is called the verb.

Sometimes verbs are called 'doing words' because they tell you what is being done in the sentence.

There is a verb in every sentence.

A Write these sentences. Choose the best verb from the brackets to fill the space.

1   We ——— a bunch of flowers from the garden.
(collected   got   picked)

2   The lame man ——— painfully along the road.
(walked   hobbled   strode)

3   Trailing smoke, the damaged plane ——— into the sea.
(plunged   fell   dropped)

4   The hounds ——— along the hedge for the fox.
(looked   hunted   searched)

B Find ten verbs in these sentences and write them in your book.

Saxon chiefs built their halls of wood. Their men felled the trees and dragged them from the forest. They trimmed off the branches with axes and split the trunks with wedges. Half trees were raised side by side to form the walls. Thatchers laid bundles of reeds on the roof and fastened them to the rafters. The women flattened the bare earth and scattered rushes to cover the floor.

This is the pinman. Write one verb to tell what he is doing in each picture.

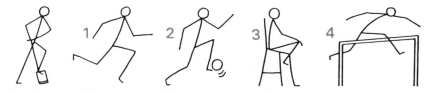

He digs.   He ———.   He ———.   He ———.   He ———.   He ———.   He ———.

Nouns with capital letters: places

Names of places always begin with capital letters.

Windy Hill

Coral Sea

Paradise Isle

Boxville

Snake River

A Write the ten nouns in this list that are names of places. Make their first letters capitals.

long london england picture wales ireland australia blue

france hundred glasgow everest belfast finger yorkshire

B Write these sentences. Give the names of people and places capital letters.

1 andrew has gone to live in oxford.

2 breda and alkmaar are in holland.

3 jean comes from ayr in scotland.

4 cardiff is the chief city of wales.

5 wembley and bow are in london.

6 italy is near france and austria.

C Write these addresses. Make all the red letters capitals.

mr james harrison,
  15, abbey street,
    west barton,
      hampshire.

dr sandra patel,
  147, ravenslea road,
    sandford park,
      manchester.

Can you find 15 place names in this line of letters? Each one begins with a red letter.

RADFORDOUGLASGOWIGANDOVEROCHESTERLINGFIELDEWSBURYEOVILFORD

Names of animals

Nouns that are names of kinds of animals begin with small letters.

A name given to an animal by its owner starts with a capital.

This dog's name is Ben.

A Write these sentences. Put in capitals where they are needed.

1 in the story, brock is a badger.

2 gwen's rabbit, peter, likes bran.

3 this pen is for lions and tigers.

4 paul's pony is called firebird.

5 the cats' names are tim and b

6 joe was chased by a huge bul

Read these sentences. Look out for names of people and animals.

Stephen and Helen Simpson went to the zoo today. The first animal they saw was a kind of antelope called an impala. Outside the bison paddock, they met Janet and Simon Willis, who took them to see two rare animals, a platypus and a panda. They stayed together for the rest of the day and had tea near the panther cage.

Copy these puzzles on squared paper. Use the names from the sentences above to complete them.

Write the names of the people here.

Write the names of the animals here.

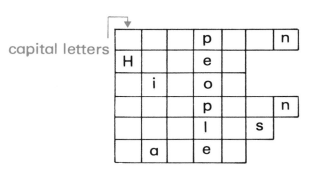

30

Collective nouns

A collective noun names a group of people or things.

a troop of monkeys

A Choose words from the box which go with these collective nouns.

a herd of ———   a fleet of ———

a bed of ———   a forest of ———

a shoal of ———   a litter of ———

a library of ———   a crew of ———

cattle	puppies	books
ships	trees	roses
fish	sailors	

B Add one letter to each of these to make the correct collective noun.

a –lass of children   a –warm of bees   an arm– of soldiers

a tea– of footballers   a –lump of trees   a crow– of people

a –and of musicians   a –ride of lions   a part– of tourists

Choose the two red words which match each black collective noun. Write them down.

Example: ⬜pack⬜ of ⬜cards⬜ or of ⬜wolves⬜ → A pack of cards or of wolves

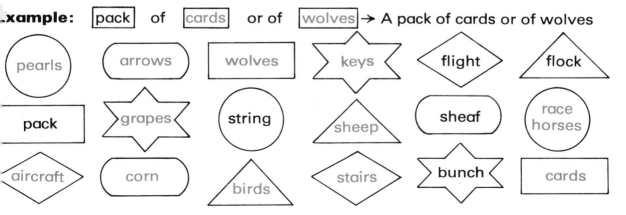

Nouns with capital letters: days, month

Names of days and months begin with capital letters.	If the words **day** or **eve** are part of a name of a special event they have a capital **D** or **E**.	**Examples:** Tuesday May St Ann's Day Wednesday

A Write these names. Make the first letter of each word a capital.

saturday june pentecost march friday february ramadan

st david's day boxing day easter sunday christmas eve

B Write each of the missing day and month names with a capital letter.

January ——— March ——— May ——— July ——— Septembe

——— November ——— Sunday ——— Tuesday ——— Thursday

C Write these sentences. Put in capital letters where they are needed.

1 new year's day is an important holiday in scotland.

2 this year, tony's birthday is on the first sunday in september.

3 the market bus goes to norwich on tuesdays and fridays.

4 in canada, most schools are on holiday in june, july and august.

5 captain yeager became the first man to break the sound barrier on tuesday, october 14th 1947.

Write the names of the special days these pictures remind you of.

 1    2    3   4   5

Plurals: words ending in y

If a word ends in a consonant followed by **y**, the plural is made by changing **y** to **ies**.

Examples:

folly → follies

dairy → dairies

hobby → hobbies

All the letters in the alphabet are consonants except for **a, e, i o, u** and **y**.

A Write the plurals of these words.

spy   army   sty   body   bully   dragonfly   melody   diary   memory
gooseberry   battery   century   brewery   boundary   lottery   galaxy

B Write plural words ending in ies to match these pictures.

C Write these sentences. Change the red words into plurals.

1. Fifty lorry carry stone from the quarry to the city.

2 The lady had poppy, pansy and lily growing in their garden.

3 In the story, the fairy stole the baby away from their family

Copy this puzzle. Use the plurals of the words in red to fill the spaces.

candy   lullaby
canary   gipsy
pasty   comedy
ruby   study   filly

		m			i	e	s
		a			i	e	s
		i			i	e	s
		l			i	e	s

	t			i	e	s
	r			i	e	s
	a			i	e	s
	i			i	e	s
	n			i	e	s

Revision

A Write these sentences. Change the red words into plurals.

Tom and Jack, the captain of the two dinghy, had won many trophy for sailing. In their own class they had both been champion. The course for the final series of race had been marked out between the two jetty. Tom took the lead at the start of the last race but ruined his chance when his boat ran into mass of seaweed.

B The words in this box are verbs. Use them to fill the spaces in the sentences below.

mended	spurted	hammered	asked	tripped	punctured

Grandma —— over the edge of the carpet. Dad —— in a nail to hold it down. A jet of water —— into the air. The nail had —— a water pipe. We —— the plumber to call. He —— the pipe.

C Write these sentences. Put in capital letters where they are needed.

1   my dog mick won a race at catford in april.

2   mr and mrs singleton are leaving for canada on thursday, september 3rd.

3   the train dawn and i caught stopped at stafford, rugby and watford.

4   marvo, the performing seal, joined the circus in may when we were at ayr.

5   during the summer, there is a bus to norwich on mondays, wednesdays, fridays and saturdays.

D Write collective nouns of your own to fill the spaces.

1 a —— of flowers   4 a —— of geese   7 a —— of cards

2 a —— of puppies   5 a —— of ships   8 a —— of cows

3 a —— of clothes   6 a —— of fish   9 a —— of bees

Just for fun

A   Divide each of these words into three smaller words.

Example: someone → so me one

together   another   cabinet   cardigan   dentistry   godfather

infantry   orator   heather   heritage   nowadays   beforehand

B   Use letters from the words in the middle to make new words for each picture.

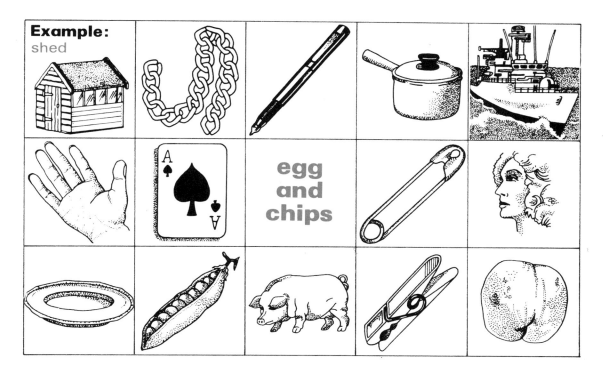

Example:
shed

egg
and
chips

C   Find the name of an animal hidden in each of these pairs of words.

Example: best oats → be(st oat)s → stoat

zinc atoms   became loyal   rinse always   rebuff alone   rich area

vestige remains   yelp ignobly   bitter attack   blaze bravely

Compound words

Compound words are made by joining two shorter words together.

Examples:

book shelf → bookshelf

screw driver → screwdriver

earth quake → earthquake

A Take a word from the black box. Add a word from the red box to make a compound word. Make fifteen compound words altogether.

gold	black	tea	water	hair
news	rain	bath	foot	green
door	cow	card	arm	wall

paper	chair	board	fish	fall
coat	boy	spoon	brush	room
house	bird	paper	ball	way

B These sentences contain twelve compound words. Write as many as you can find. Then write the two words which form the compound word in each case.

All afternoon, the thunderstorm raged along the mountainside. Black rainclouds blotted out the skyline. By nightfall, the steady downpour had turned the rainwater gulleys into raging torrents. Floodwater cascaded from the hillside above the farmhouse and carried away the cowsheds.

Copy the crossword on to squared paper. Use the picture clues to find compound words to solve the puzzle.

1 across

1 down

2 down

3 down

4 down

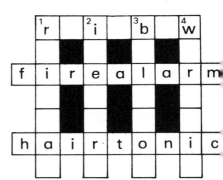

Simple sentences

A simple sentence makes a statement or asks a question about one thing.

A simple sentence contains only one verb.

Example:

The big fish swims in the deep pool.

A These are simple sentences. Write the verb from each one.
The verb is the word that tells you what is being done.

1   Peter broke the window again.

2   Young puppies chase their tails.

3   I sold him that old chair.

4   Strong winds uproot tall trees.

5   The kite drifted across the field.

6   Jim wrote a letter to you.

7   Terry laughed at the joke.

8   Never go near the lions.

9   Bad news travels fast.

10 His family lives in Bristol.

B Put spaces between these words and add full stops to make them into simple sentences.

1   Takethisheavyboxdownstairswithyouafterdinner   (one sentence)

2   Inspringtimethebirdsbuildnests   (one sentence)

Write a simple sentence about each picture.

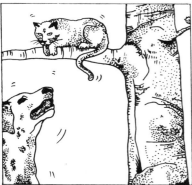

Sentences: subject and object

Most simple sentences have a subject and an object. Subjects and objects are nouns.

The subject tells you who or what the sentence is about.

The object tells you who or what is having something done to it.

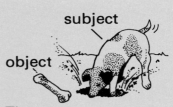

subject

object

The **puppy** buries a **bone.**

A Write the subject (one word) of each of these sentences.

1 Elephants carry heavy logs.

2 Ostriches have long legs.

3 Peter met my brother today.

4 He dug a trench for the beans.

5 Birds like the summertime.

B Write the object (one word) of each of these sentences.

1 We are planting trees.

2 Diane is drinking milk.

3 All the players won medals.

4 Simon pushed me down the stairs.

5 The old horse pulled barges along the canal.

Write a sentence about each picture. Make the part of the picture labelled S the subject and the part labelled O the object.

Long and short sentences

A sentence can be as long or as short as you choose to make it.

Long sentences are often used to describe places or people.

Short, brisk sentences are useful for describing exciting happenings.

A Read this passage.

As he wandered aimlessly along the narrow forest path, the wild boar stopped here and there to root out the juicy underground stems of the obanche vine, which grows a metre a day in the hot, steamy dankness of the deep jungle. Suddenly, he stopped. His nose twitched. He turned in an instant and crashed away through the dark undergrowth.

1 How many sentences are there?

2 How many words are there in the longest sentence?

3 How many words are there in the shortest sentence?

B Put spaces between these words and add full stops to make them into sentences.

1 SmokepouredfromtheroofFlamesshotfromthewindowSomeone criedforhelp   (three sentences)

2 Thetinycottagesleptpeacefullybeneathathickblanketofcrispsnow (one sentence)

Write four short sentences to describe what is happening in these pictures.

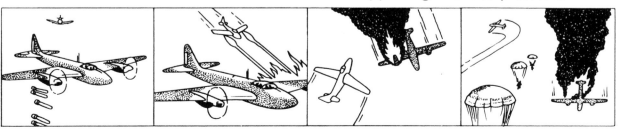

Making opposites: un

Some words can be made into their opposites by putting **un** in front of them.

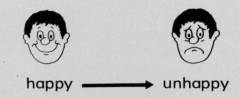

happy ⟶ unhappy

A   Write un in front of these words.

safe   sure   dress   clean   broken   common   like   holy

pack   tie   well   even   locks   load   noticed   employed

B   Write these sentences. Use one of the opposites you have just made to fill each space.

1   I cannot —— my shoelace.

2   Help me to —— this parcel.

3   The small key —— this door.

4   The eagle is a most —— bird.

5   It took four men to —— the piano

6   The footpath is broken and ——.

7   The bomb lay —— in the corner.

8   David felt —— after eating the pie

C   All of these words begin with un but only ten of them are opposites of other words. Write the ten.

undress   until   unfit   uncover   uncle   untrue   underwear   unit

underline   unwise   unicorn   unjust   unpleasant   unpopular   unable

undone

Take the last letter of each word you have just written. Put the letters together, in the order you see them above, to make the names of two things shown in this picture.

40

Singular and plural: is, are, was, were

After a singular word, write **is** or **was**. After a plural, write **are** or **were**.

Examples:

is: are

He is here.

They are here.

was: were

The door was shut.

The doors were shut.

A Write these words in two lists, headed SINGULAR and PLURAL.

car   cars   man   women   jar   house   she   we   clocks   nurses

field   woods   pencil   bells   bushes   day   caravans   windmill

B Write these sentences. Use is or are to fill each space.

1   Tim —— always late.

2   Alan and Elizabeth —— twins.

3   This —— your last chance.

4   This —— the nine o'clock news.

C Write these sentences. Use was or were to fill each space.

1   The leaves —— falling.

2   Mrs Reid's windows —— dirty.

3   There I ——, trapped in the cave!

4   That —— the last bus.

D Write these sentences. Use is, are, was and were once each to fill the spaces.

Yesterday, I —— a thousand miles away. Mum, Dad, my sister and I —— on holiday in Spain. We —— looking forward to going again next year. Dad says that, after Christmas, he —— going to start saving for next year's holiday.

Can you find is, are, was and were hidden in this line of letters?

washaredrawereadish

'Helper' verbs

Look at these sentences.

A   He **is** the Chief Scout.

B   He **is** going to school.

In sentence A, **is** stands alone as the verb.

In sentence B, **is** forms part of the main verb.

In sentence B, **is** is a 'helper' or auxiliary verb. Here are some more 'helper' verbs.

am   are   was   were   has

had   must   may   shall   will

can   could   should   would

might

A   Pick out the 'helper' verbs from these sentences.

1   I am taking the window out.

2   They are swimming in the sea.

3   He was buying some fireworks.

4   Jean will wait for you outside.

5   Father has ordered a greenhouse.

6   We must buy some eggs.

B   Write these sentences. Use am, is, are, was or were to fill each space.

1   I —— leaving the twins at home when I go away.

2   They —— picking all the apples some time next week.

3   A man —— coming to mend the washer tomorrow afternoon.

C   Write these sentences. Use shall, can, would or must to fill each space.

1   We —— have to wait and see what happens next.

2   Susan —— play almost any tune on her recorder.

3   Joe —— like to join the swimming club when he is older.

Find eight different auxiliary ('helper') verbs which could be used to fill this space.

John —— learn to swim.

Shortened words

In everyday speech some pairs of words are run together.

Example:

I am → I'm
he is → he's

We write these joined pairs of words only in letters to friends or when writing down words that have been spoken.

A comma written above the line shows where the letter should be.

A Write these joined pairs in full. **Example:** wasn't → was not

1 we're 2 she's 3 they're 4 don't 5 mustn't

6 didn't 7 wouldn't 8 couldn't 9 doesn't 10 shouldn't

B Write these sentences. Join the pairs of red words together.
Write a comma above the line to mark the position of the missing letter.

Example: John is coming home today. → John's coming home today.

1 "The baker is not coming this week," Susan said.

2 I have not forgotten what you did while I was away.

3 Do you think it is a long way from here to London?

4 "Has not he written yet?" Barbara asked angrily.

5 "Who is the owner of this coat?" Miss Martin demanded.

6 Mother said that you are not to go there again.

Copy the puzzle on to squared paper. Join each of these pairs of words and fit them into the puzzle.

I am   he is   she is   did not

must not   could not   should not

Plural nouns: irregular

Some words change their forms in the plural.

Examples:

child → children   woman → women

man → men   mouse → mice   ox → oxen

goose → geese   tooth → teeth   foot → feet

A   Change all the red words into plurals.

The little mouse crept under the big double door. In the dim corner of the stable, gentle ox patiently chewed the cud. Goose were asleep in the straw, head tucked under snowy wing. Woman from the village clustered around the cradle and laid their gift at his foot.

Out of the tooth-chattering cold of the winter night came three wise man. They sank to their knee and worshipped the child of all child, the baby of all baby, the king of all king.

B   Write these sentences, choosing the correct word from the brackets.

1   The geese (is   are) near the pond.

2   One man (is   are) running away.

3   Oxen (is   are) pulling the plough.

4   Oats (is   are) grown in this field.

5   The mice (is   are) making a nest.

6   Children (is   are) charged half fare.

Choose plurals from the list at the top of the page to fit these pictures.

1

2

3

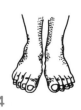
4

5

Verbs: past, present and future

Verbs can tell you about:

Something that
has already
happened=**past**

Example:

He walked home.
He was walking home.

Something that
is happening
now=**present**

Example:

He walks home.
He is walking home.

Something that is yet
to happen=**future**

Example:

He will walk home.

A Read these sentences. Write their numbers. Put past, present or future
after each number.

1 I saw Mrs O'Hara this morning.

2 I see a car arriving now.

3 I shall see them next week.

4 There will be a practice later.

5 The bottom fell out of the boat.

6 They are waiting for Gwen.

7 Did he tell you about the tickets?

8 Jane swam two lengths today.

9 Is Peter at home today?

10 Will you go to Margate this year?

B Write these sentences as though they had happened in the past.

1 Peter wears a blue tie.

2 I shall leave school at Easter.

3 The soldiers are driving trucks.

4 Mr Worrall works at the station.

5 Bears roam in the forest.

6 They will have to wait outside.

Look at these pictures and decide whether they belong to the past, the present or
the future. Write their numbers or draw them and, next to each one, write past,
present or future.

1   2   3   4   5

Revision

A   Look at this simple sentence.   **The brown fox caught a rabbit.**

Answer these questions.

A   What is the subject of the sentence?

B   Which word (or words) makes up the verb?

C   What is the object of the sentence?

D   Does the sentence tell you about the past, the present or the future?

Now answer the same four questions for each of the sentences numbered 1 to 4.
Example: Friendly Indians helped the settlers.

Answers: A   Friendly Indians   B   helped   C   the settlers   D   past

1   John has taken the letters.   3   They are finishing their homework.

2   A heavy lorry hit the bridge.   4   Dogs grow thick coats in winter.

B   Write words beginning with un which mean:

not fit   sad   not safe   dirty   not fastened   foolish   not popular   ill

not usual   false   not pleasant   rough   not loaded   without clothes

C   Write the plurals of:

kiss   woman   child   ferry   goose   ox   box   mouse   house

remedy   tooth   gas   berry   boot   foot   compass   plate   bus

D   Write these sentences. Choose the correct word from the brackets.

1   Lions (were   was) prowling all night.

2   Television has (to   too) many repeats.

3   Simon jumped (of   off) the bed.

4   The king of spades (is   are) here.

Just for fun

A Can you find fifteen things in the picture with names ending in t?

B Arrange these words into sentences by writing the shortest word first, then the next shortest and so on to the longest word, which will be last.

1 pastries you do Belgian cream like filled?

2 best woman election I seeking am the worker

3 small written is properly only m the letter

C Make a sentence by reading the words in the red grid. The word order is shown in the black grid. **Example:** 1 the 2 otter

The	a	in	lives
called	the	otter	a
water	holt	near	den

1	8	7	3
10	5	2	11
6	12	4	9

D Read every second letter to find out what this says.

y t l h x e s b n l o u w e c w a h k a j l t e d i r s l t y h r e g b h i o g z g r e

d s i t b l o i g v e i f n h g t c x r m e w a r t y u v r w e

Index